FORGOTTEN
VIRGINIA

FORGOTTEN
VIRGINIA

ABANDONED PLACES AND THINGS
IN THE OLD DOMINION

SEAN TOLER

AMERICA
THROUGH TIME®
ADDING COLOR TO AMERICAN HISTORY

*Dedicated to Natalie, Lainee-bug, Brady-boy,
and Loganito—my inspiration.*

America Through Time is an imprint of Fonthill Media LLC
www.through-time.com
office@through-time.com

Published by Arcadia Publishing by arrangement with Fonthill Media LLC
For all general information, please contact Arcadia Publishing:
Telephone: 843-853-2070
Fax: 843-853-0044
E-mail: sales@arcadiapublishing.com
For customer service and orders:
Toll-Free 1-888-313-2665

www.arcadiapublishing.com

First published 2020

Copyright © Sean Toler 2020

ISBN 978-1-63499-226-8

Typeset in Trade Gothic 10pt on 15pt
Printed and bound in England

CONTENTS

Introduction   **7**

1   The Roots of My Abandonment Photography   **9**

2   General Abandonment   **14**

3   Specific Locations   **79**

About the Author   **96**

INTRODUCTION

I t is difficult these days to go on a drive without seeing at least one deserted and abandoned home or building. While many people may view them as blights on the scenery, there are others—myself included—who see them as much more. Within the walls of these buildings took place countless stories that now go untold, numberless memories now long forgotten. Though a lot of these stories may now only live in the past, the buildings themselves still remain, for now. This is one of the reasons why I began photographing old buildings—to try and do my part to preserve them in time, before they are no longer around.

In the pages of this book, you will find photographs of some of the many abandoned places and things I have come across throughout the years. I have also included backstories and any history I have been able to uncover about these places. I hope, as you read, that you will come to appreciate these old edifices for the beauty they still possess, even as they seemingly struggle to retain the strength and composure that has ever so slowly slipped from their grasp.

1

THE ROOTS OF MY ABANDONMENT PHOTOGRAPHY

If I had to determine a starting point in my love of photographing old, abandoned buildings, it would probably be a result of pictures not taken that I now regret not having photographed. As a teenager in the early 1990s, I worked at an old country store. This building itself was well along in its years and lifespan at the time. It sat across the street from the farm once owned by my great-great-grandparents and their nineteen children (they had a total of twenty-one, but two were stillborn). The farmhouse itself had once been a store/motel used by travelers in the days of horse-and-buggy travel; I am sure the fact that it had all of those rooms came in very handy for a family raising nineteen children. In 2012, I went out to that old farm and photographed what still stood. I have not been there since, but I have heard it is no longer possible to reach the property in a vehicle. The two photographs on the next page show what was left standing of the old farmhouse, when I was there in 2012.

Also on the old farm were a few barns I have heard quite a few stories about from my grandfather (he also grew up on the farm). I was honestly surprised that they were still standing when I took the two shots on page 11.

A little way away from the main farmhouse, up a hill behind these two barns sat a smaller home. My great-grandparents lived in this home, and when my grandfather and my grandmother first got married, they lived on the second floor of this home (see page 12).

The old building that once was the home of my great-great grandparents and their nineteen children. Before that, it was a store called Bowles Store.

The back of the old home. The Corvair in the picture once belonged to my late great-great uncle.

The old barns that remain on the property.

One of the old barns that remain on the property.

An old home on the property where my great-grandparents and grandparents once lived.

On that day in 2012, I also saw the van pictured at the top of page 13. Someone had recently spent a lot of time clearing away some of the brush that had grown up all around it. I remember seeing this van sitting in that spot as a child, back when the farmhouse was still very much intact. The story, as related to me by my father, is that one day, a gentleman drove it up to the farm and asked my great-uncle if he could leave it there for a few days. The gentleman never returned. When I took this photo, the van was still parked in the same spot where that unknown gentleman had left it all those years before.

Sitting right next door to the old country store where I worked as a teenager were two much older and worn buildings, one of which had at one time been an apartment in which my grandparents had lived for a few years when my father was born. In the mid-1990s, the eventual demise of the old store materialized as a brand-new gas station, convenience store, and fast food restaurant that was built just up the road. It did not take long at all for the old country store to be run out of business by this new competitor. Unfortunately, I never photographed the old store nor the adjacent buildings. While I was across the country at college, the buildings were demolished. Now, a guardrail sits where the entrance to the parking lot once was, and it is impossible to tell that the store even once sat in that spot. In fact, only the building pictured at the bottom of page 13 (which sat a little way off to the side and behind it in the woods) was the only clue that anything had ever been there at all. Sadly however, less than a year after I shot this photo, this building was reduced to a pile of rubble from a tree that fell on it during a storm.

The old van once left behind by a gentleman who said he would return in a few days to pick it up. He never did return though.

After enlarging this photo, I was able to make out the words "Oilville Motor" on the front of the building. This must have, at one time, been a repair garage. This building no longer stands.

2

GENERAL ABANDONMENT

For many years, when I was still single, I felt the urge to venture out on the weekends to look for old, abandoned buildings and photograph them with my point-and-shoot digital camera. I now regret never having acted on those urges. It was not until I was gifted a new DSLR camera for Christmas one year by my father-in-law that I began to get serious about photography. Now, with a wife and three young children, all of that time I had as a single man has mostly disappeared, though I would never trade what I have now for all of that missed free time.

The building on the next page is the first abandoned building I ever photographed. In its prime, it was a post office. For most of my life, it sat as you see it in this photo. Sadly, however, it now no longer exists. A year or two after I took this photo, it sustained significant damage during a storm; the owners decided at that point to have it demolished.

On many occasions, I have been asked if I ever go inside of the buildings I photograph. For most of them the answer is "No" mostly because of very visible "No Trespassing" signs. There is also another reason why I mostly do not enter, which goes back to my childhood. One day, myself, my brother, and our friend were playing in the woods down the road from our houses when we came across what appeared to be an outdoor workbench built by someone many years in the past. There were lots of random items scattered around on the ground, some of which were long fluorescent light bulbs. We then noticed the old abandoned house sitting nearby. We decided that we wanted to see what was inside the house, but the door was locked. The locked door was easily remedied by a swift roundhouse kick performed by one of us (I will refrain from saying which one of us, however). At the time, we were disappointed as there was nothing inside that was "cool". Of course, now I would consider it a treasure trove of photographic opportunities, but anything found would remain.

The old Vontay post office. This building no longer stands.

I now like to follow the adage I learned as a young boy scout: "Take only photographs, leave only footprints." So, we left the house and went back out to the old workbench and decided it would be fun to throw the fluorescent bulbs against trees to break them. As I said earlier, we noticed the old house. What we had failed to notice was the newer, lived-in house on the other side of the old house. It did not take long for our ruckus to attract the attention of the homeowner next door who began walking towards us. Once we saw him, we fled—myself in one direction and my brother and our friend in the opposite direction. As I found out later, when I returned home to find a sheriff's deputy sitting in our driveway, the man had followed my brother and our friend. They had fled a little way and had attempted to hide beneath a large cedar tree. They got caught. Due to that experience, I believe, I always feel very hesitant about entering into abandoned buildings. There are, as I said before, times when I do enter but I can count those instances on one hand. The following photographs are from one of those times.

This is an historic home that was stripped and relocated in the name of progress. At this house, there was no sign to be found, and the door sat wide open. I also always worry about the strength of the aged timbers in old buildings like this, but I will say, though this house was more than 200 years old, I never heard a single board creak beneath me as I walked through it. I have noticed lately, though, work is now beginning to be done to this old home.

This building was once maintained as an historical site until it was relocated in the name of progress.

I have often wondered what various scenes of everyday life once played out in now lonely rooms such as these. Of this next room, in particular, I like to imagine the excited footsteps of joyous children rushing down these stairs to see what surprises awaited them under the tree on Christmas morning.

With the stress we all face in our day-to-day lives, it is only natural to want a place where we can go to escape, to just get away from it all—maybe to an empty room in an empty house, with a soft, well-worn chair in front of a window through which we can gaze while daydreaming of happier times—a window that then becomes our very own window to the past.

Many people have asked me over the years how I come across the old buildings that I photograph. My answer to them is this: I go out in my car and drive and purposely get myself lost in search of them. I have found that I cannot hope to uncover as yet undiscovered locations if I am not willing to venture down roads on which I have never before traveled.

The stairs inside the previously pictured home.

One of the downstairs rooms in the previously pictured home.

One of the upstairs rooms in the previously pictured home. This chair was already positioned like this when I discovered it.

An old business in a rural town.

An old service station. If it were not for the sign, I would have assumed this was someone's house.

Another old house along a country road.

This old home still had an old outhouse behind it.

Does anyone else see the irony in having a sign that reads "Antiques Ahead" on a building that is itself an antique?

An old business that now sits empty along a busy stretch of highway.

An old truck sits in front of a now unused building that was once part of a roadside motel.

This is one of the most iconic abandoned homes in the state. I bet it was a beautiful sight to see when it was new.

Whenever I see old porches such as these on abandoned houses, I try to imagine what life must have been like in much simpler times. I picture people sitting out on these porches in the cool of the evening or on a warm spring day, enjoying their surroundings and spending time together as a family. Now, these porches sit as empty as the houses they adorn. One can almost sense that they still sit, patiently longing for the feel of rocking chairs swaying back and forth on their now decayed timbers once again.

I titled this one "Memories of the old Sitting Porch." This home no longer stands.

I assume this was a business at one time, but as I have seen in many other instances, it could have also been someone's home.

This looks to me like more of a home than a business. There must have been a rocking chair or two on this porch at one time or another.

Another one of the most iconic abandoned homes in the state. I have been told this house once was a home for boys, a brothel, as well as someone's house (not at the same time obviously).

Nature is well on its way to reclaiming this old home.

This was the first print I ever sold. A lady in Michigan purchased it as a birthday gift for her father whom she said grew up in this house.

This house looks as though it came straight out of a horror movie.

This house most definitely predates the interstate that lies next to it.

This old home almost went unnoticed as I was driving by. I never went inside, but for some reason the urge to do so has never left me.

I often wonder how much time has passed since homes like this were lived in.

The longer you stare at this house the more confusing it gets.

A friend of mine tipped me off about this house. The day that I took this photo, a lady came walking down the driveway and told me that her father had grown up in this home.

The well-worn door that you see next leads to what was once the kitchen of the humble home shown after. One can only imagine the enticing aromas that at one time may have permeated the air as fresh meals and goodies were prepared within these walls. I was told by the gentleman living next door that when this home was livable, two elderly ladies resided here. I can almost picture them coming into the kitchen door with their aprons pulled up, full of fresh vegetables from the garden that would soon be incorporated into tasty meals.

This home shown on page 31 was once the farmhouse on what is now an abandoned farm. I do not expect it, or the other buildings on this property, to remain standing for very much longer as the "progress" of commercial development is quite literally on the doorstep.

Left: I love this old door. I even brought my young children here so they could sit on this step for a photoshoot.

Below: I wish I could have photographed this home before part of the second floor collapsed.

The old farmhouse. I have often wondered what life was like on this old farm.

An old chicken coop on the same farm as the farmhouse in the previous photo.

One of the sadder things I have noticed as I have driven around the back country roads of Virginia is the number of farms that now sit abandoned and unused. Once full of life and activity, they are now a symbol of the times in which we live where everything needs to be delivered immediately and so much of our food comes from factories and processing plants.

I am quite fond of the photo of the abandoned store shown at the bottom of page 39. It makes me think of days gone by when cars may have been worked on in the back part of the building, while locals would stop by to purchase a quick something or just to chat. Old country stores like these are getting harder and harder to find, especially ones that are still open and operational. I also love it because it reminds me of the one I spoke of earlier, where I worked as a teenager.

An old barn that has seen better days.

This is a very unique-looking barn in the mountains of Western Virginia.

An old farmhouse with an old tractor still parked next to it. This home no longer stands.

Abandoned barns and silos on an abandoned farm.

Another abandoned farmhouse. I did not notice the buzzards on the roof when I was taking the photo.

Above: The barn that sits behind the house in the previous photo.

Right: An abandoned grain silo that sits all alone in the middle of a field.

Yet more abandoned farm buildings.

An old barn sitting in a recently harvested field.

An abandoned farm in Eastern Virginia.

An abandoned barn that was part of an abandoned farm that was later turned into a golf course. When I took this photo, the golf course was abandoned as well. Now all of the buildings are gone.

Just another in what seems like an endless display of abandoned barns and farms.

I love the look of this old barn.

The farm on which this barn resides is far from abandoned, but this barn has definitely seen better days. I drove past it recently and saw that it has sustained even more damage.

The old Winterpock Grocery store.

In this day and age of big box stores, convenience, and "progress," I feel that we are actually digressing as the history all around us is abandoned, forgotten, demolished, or left to rot.

As I have driven around, not only on my outings dedicated to searching out abandonment, but just everyday errands, I have discovered items other than buildings and houses that have seemingly been left behind as well.

An old general store on its way back to nature.

A former store in the town called Forks of Buffalo.

I do not know what the original purpose of this building was, but it has sat looking like this for most of my life.

An old abandoned store. The text on the front reads "Hasty Mini Mart."

This was an old handmade chair that used to sit down the road from my house. Not long after taking this photo, the chair disappeared and has never returned.

"Wheels of Misfortune."

"Stationary Wagon."

Part of the old Petersburg Ironworks.

Another part of the old ironworks.

A wagon sitting in front of an abandoned farmhouse.

Yet it is my love of these old buildings that drives me to get out in search of them because I know that the clock is always ticking. In the same way that our own houses feel like home to us, you can be sure that someone at some point in time must have felt the same about these old houses and buildings. People lived there, worked there, spent their whole lives there, and maybe even died in these edifices. It is a shame to think that the events that took place in them should be forgotten and the buildings themselves be lost to the ravages of time.

However, the more of these abandoned places I find, the more I realize that the story remains unchanged. Still they sit, unoccupied, unused, unlived-in, and unremembered.

An old abandoned duplex in Petersburg.

An old water treatment building.

An old shed with a long-retired plow sitting in front of it.

This sits across the street from a church, so I assume it was once the church itself or an outbuilding.

The remains of a school that has not seen children walking its halls in many a year.

Another old country store that has not been open for quite a while.

An old store once called Schall's.

A tiny little home on the side of a busy road.

An old building that sits behind a church.

The old Rocketts Mill House in Hanover County.

I nearly missed this house while driving by. It was well off the road and I had to use my zoom lens to get a decent shot.

Above: Another home that required me to pull out the zoom lens.

Right: A very unique-looking home tucked away in a small town.

This next home is the second abandoned house I have entered. I only went as far as the front of the house. I am always wondering what might be lurking in the shadows of an old, unused building; it is probably best to not find out.

There are happy outcomes once in a while. Not every abandoned building is doomed to slowly decay it seems. The building pictured at the bottom of page 54 sat just as it is in this photo for as long as I can remember. It is located at the edge of the town of Ashland and served as a reminder of days long past. However, recently, its owners invested heavily in restoring it and turning it into a neighborhood restaurant that has been very successful since the day it opened, and one, I might add, that serves very delicious food.

This church pictured on page 55 seems to have become a success story as well. This photo represents the way it looked for many years. However, recently, it has been restored and turned into a wedding chapel.

This little home will certainly be demolished soon as there is commercial development on all sides.

The garage/shed at the previous pictured home.

Someone at one time enjoyed sitting in the living room while playing records on this old record player.

What is left of the living room in the previous pictured house. It looks as though someone came looking for copper pipes to remove from the walls.

If you are ever in Ashland, be sure to stop by Jake's Place to have a bite to eat.

For many years, this church sat as though it was waiting for its congregation to return. Now it has been restored and functions as a wedding chapel.

It is nice to know that at least some of the buildings I have photographed are no longer on an ever so slow journey to their demise.

I wish I could say that only these buildings are all that gets abandoned and forgotten in today's world, but unfortunately, I cannot. In many cases, the ones who may have lived or worked in these buildings end up all alone as they live out the lonely final years of their lives.

Just as we do now, they too once had lives full of careers, friends, and families. The events of their lives may now seem to us to have taken place long ago, but to them (and it will be the same for ourselves all too soon), they happened only yesterday.

The blooming flowers in the tree nicely offset the decay of this old beauty.

An old shed or garage peeking out from the overgrown brush that surrounds it.

This church is no longer used as a church, but I have since learned it is not necessarily abandoned. Still, it has a look that makes you want to stop and take a closer look if it were not for all of the "no trespassing" signs that abound.

The faded writing at the top of the side of this building reads "Thompson's Store." My zoom lens came in handy for this shot as well.

An abandoned home that I have recently learned was once the home of the uncle of a friend's husband.

An old shed on the side of the previously pictured house.

An old barn that I spotted at the edge of the woods as I was driving by.

Further into the woods was this building. I am not sure what its purpose ever was as I could not find a door nor a window anywhere on it.

They possess the wisdom of a lifetime and are the storytellers for our generation. They can bring life, once again, to the aged structures that lie all around us through the passing along of their history and the telling of the tales of their lives. We can, with a little bit of time and attention, in turn bring life to them once again.

The old home shown on page 63 is one in which I attempted to enter. Unfortunately, it did not work out as I had hoped. As I drove around on back country roads one Saturday, I passed by this house and caught a glimpse of it as I drove by. I immediately found a place to safely turn around and went back to it. It sat about 100 yards off of the road and any semblance of a driveway that may have once been present had long been replaced by soil and undergrowth. I pulled my car in and got out. I found a good angle and set up my camera and tripod and got the shot pictured next. Once I had gotten my shots, I decided to investigate a little more closely. The front door was no longer attached. There had obviously once been a front porch because the front doorway was several feet above ground level.

An abandoned church near the town of Beaverdam.

An old mill near Culpeper.

The writing on this old building reads "C & W Restaurant." As I photographed it, I could imagine the neon signs on the front all aglow on a Saturday night with cars filling the parking lot and diners filling the tables.

I would be willing to bet that most if not all of these trees did not exist the last time this house was lived in.

Someone had taken the front door and laid it down so that it acted as a ramp to walk up to enter the house.

Having not seen any "No Trespassing" signs, I decided that I was going to go inside and see if I could get some good interior shots. I took a first step onto the door and everything seemed fine. The second step let me know otherwise, however. When my foot came down onto the door in my second step, the typical solid feeling of a good sturdy door had been replaced by a soft mushy sort of feeling. This feeling quickly gave way to a feeling of there being nothing below my foot, and then again, that feeling gave way to the feeling of my foot making contact with the ground. The problem was that this had caused me to lose my balance, and I ended up being bent over backwards as though I were in a limbo competition with my right leg caught all the way up to my hip in the remnants of a now seemingly ancient front door. I quickly looked around for something I could grab hold of so I could pull myself up and get my leg out of the door. There was plenty to grab hold of around me; unfortunately, all of it was sapling trees with zero rigidity. I then remembered my tripod that I was still somehow holding onto. I used it to brace myself and was able to get myself upright and withdraw my leg from the door. It was then that I reassessed my desire to go inside of that house and turned away from it, returning to my car and leaving. I have since attempted to locate this house on Google Maps satellite view and have discovered that it has been restored.

The home that made me rethink my desire to go inside. This house has been restored and is now being lived in once again.

The photo at the top of the next page at first glance does not seem like anything more than a typical fast food place that has gone out of business. For me, however, it reminds me of my childhood. Once upon a time, this was a Dairy Queen. My parents used to take us here once in a while. Beneath the Dairy Queen was another business. At the back of the restaurant were some booths with windows overlooking a large back parking lot area for the business below. I think it was a repair place that serviced big diesel engines because there were always buses and tractor trailers down in that parking lot. On one occasion, my brother and I were looking down and saw a tractor trailer with a wind deflector on top of the cab. These were still somewhat new at that time, and my brother and I talked about how cool it would be to sneak down and climb up the cab and stow away behind the wind deflector and ride across the country. That is what I see when I look at this picture: two young brothers about to eat lunch with their family, awed by the big trucks out of the window with their imaginations running wild.

The three photos that follow the one described above are of the only other house into which I have entered. This time, however, it was with full permission from the owner. The family building a house on this property discovered this old gem next to the new house, a few yards into the woods. There is no telling how long it has been standing there or how long it has been abandoned, but one thing is for sure: whoever once lived there had to have been tiny in order to get up those oddly placed stairs to the second floor. I am very grateful that I was given the chance to capture it on camera while it still stands.

This was at one time a Dairy Queen and later was a Sbarro Pizza. It is only a matter of time before it is just a memory.

An old country home discovered by the new landowners while building a new home on the property.

The side door of the same house. I am not sure if the fireplace was meant to be an outdoor fireplace or if there was once another portion of this house that has been lost to time.

The inside of the same house. I did not even consider trying to go up those stairs to photograph the second floor.

Lately, as I have traveled around looking for these abandoned beauties, I have noticed a strange thing happening—I have noticed a feeling of sadness that lingers with me for a few days after each outing. As my mind dwells on these now long empty buildings, I almost feel as if my imagination is transported back to when their walls were filled with life and laughter (I never imagine anything bad happened within them as that would just make the sadness I feel that much more unbearable). For a small moment, these now aged piles of timbers are instantly transformed to the pinnacle of their glory days, almost like a flashback in a movie or television show. Before my mind's eye, I see scenes played out of what it might have been like long ago before those who dwelt or worked within these buildings closed their doors one last time, never to return. Then, almost as instantly as the flashback began, it fades back to the solemn reality lying before me and the feelings of emptiness and abandonment also come rushing back. How sad it is to know that these buildings once embodied the dreams and pride of those who came before us but now are hardly even noticed by those passing by. I wish I could get out and get every old abandoned place photographed properly and even learn the history behind them before nature reclaims them or they suffer destruction from the cold, blunt steel of heavy equipment.

A cozy little home that is slowly becoming part of the woods.

A lovely old home next to railroad tracks in a quiet little town.

A country club now surrounds this beautiful and elegant old home.

This little home was hiding behind some other buildings, but fortunately, I turned my head in time to spot it as I drove by.

I hope the train does not still come through there or whoever built that fence is going to be angry.

I cannot tell what this building may have been used for in its prime.

This old store sits right next to the building in the previous photo.

Another old store left abandoned.

The old Lucks Feed and Seed building in Beaverdam.

Francisco's Store. I have been told that this building has also been restored.

This is why I, and so many others like myself, venture out whenever we are able seeking out these decrepit treasures—we hope that by photographing them that we are, in our own way, preserving them for future generations to behold when the time will long be passed to view them in person. Nothing beats the feeling of excitement and awe that we experience each time we discover another decaying building. It is as if the buildings themselves have been calling to us, preserving their final bit of strength until we have had the chance to document that they did, indeed, once exist and, in many cases, were glorious in their prime. Every single one represents a piece of our history, and once they have disappeared from the landscape, in most cases, so has their history.

I am guessing this was an old strip mall at one time. Honestly, to me it looks more like part of an old western town.

One could barely notice this farmhouse peeking through the trees when I took this photo. It has since been demolished.

An old shed sitting next to a busy stretch of road.

This sits right next to the old shed in the previous photo. New housing developments are going in rapidly in the area surrounding it.

An old barn on an abandoned farm. The last I heard, the farmland had been sold and a housing development was being built on the land.

An old abandoned farmhouse.

This is the back side of the house in the previous photo.

An old home in a quiet suburb. The last time I drove by, it appeared as though this home had been demolished.

Sitting next to a busy road, this old beauty is nearly impossible to see until the trees lose their leaves in the fall.

It will not be much longer until this old home is completely swallowed up by the encroaching trees.

3

SPECIFIC LOCATIONS

In a remote section of Virginia, out among farms and rolling countryside lies the abandoned ghost town of Union Level.

As I was driving out to this location, I marveled at the fact that there was indeed nothing around this small little stretch of what used to be an up-and-coming town. I thought that it was a very strange place for a town to develop as there are no bodies of water nearby, or a railroad, or anything that would cause a community to settle and flourish in this spot. As I started researching its history, I discovered that there actually was a railroad here once upon a time. In fact, there were as many as twenty businesses in town in the early 1900s. In the mid-1800s, this town was founded on the horse and carriage line. Later on, in the late 1800s and on into the 1980s, it was a stop on the rail line. Sometime in the mid-1980s the railroad was abandoned, and later on, in the 1990s, the post office closed, which, in turn, meant the impending demise of this once bustling town. I am not certain at what point the last business closed its doors, but there is an old gas station with a gas pump out front that reads $0.36 per gallon.

Above: The town of Union Level.

Left: One of the old buildings in Union Level.

Another building in Union Level.

Union Level, VA.

Union Level, VA.

Union Level, VA.

Union Level, VA.

Union Level, VA.

Approximately 60 miles to the northwest of Union Level is another similar town known as Pamplin City. I would not go as far as to say that it is a ghost town as well, as there is still a lot of activity in this little town, but the ten buildings that lie on its main street certainly resemble one. The town was named after the gentleman who donated land for the railroad that would run right through the town. Due to the arrival of the railroad, the town prospered—so much so that its name was changed to Pamplin City. It is not known exactly when people began settling in this spot, but it was long before the 1850s when this name change occurred. At one point, the main street was adorned with hotels and shops, while beautifully ornate homes were built around the town. At one point, Pamplin was home to the largest producer of clay smoking pipes in the world. In its prime, the facility was producing 1 million pipes per month. Sadly though, as rail travel began to decline, so did this little town. There have been recent efforts to revitalize portions of the town. One such example is the former train depot that was fixed up and repurposed as an annex for the Appomattox County Library. As I drove into town to take these shots, I was easily able to imagine the hustle and bustle that once took place in the town as old locomotives arrived at, and departed from, the former little depot.

Above left: One of the buildings in Pamplin City.

Above right: Another building in Pamplin City.

Right: Pamplin City, VA.

Above and below left: Pamplin City, VA.

Below right: This is the side of one of the buildings in Pamplin City. I discovered this by accident but I am quite happy that I did.

The next photo is by far the most popular one I have ever photographed. It has made its way around the internet by various means; in fact, it often shows up on my Pinterest feed as an item in which I may be interested. Little does Pinterest know that it is showing me my own photograph. This particular photograph is one of the buildings from the old abandoned renaissance faire. I have been told that this building served as "Rapunzel's Tower."

Rapunzel's tower in the old abandoned renaissance faire.

The two photos that follow this one were taken on the same piece of property. From 1996 to 1999, this place attracted many, filling their days with food, fun, and a medieval experience. Now, the buildings sit unused and empty as trees and undergrowth ever so slowly reclaim them. On the day I captured these images, a group of us had decided to travel to this location in hopes of getting some good photographs of the old and, frankly, very unique buildings on this property. We were dismayed to find that the access roads were gated shut and there were an abundance of "No Trespassing" signs on display. As we stood there bemoaning our fate, we heard the sound of a vehicle approaching us from within the property. Soon, a pickup truck came around a bend and stopped at the gate where we were standing. We asked the occupants if we could go onto the property and photograph the old buildings. To our very pleasant surprise, we were given permission and were told to make sure we locked the gate when we left. We were ecstatic. So, in we went and began what would be a few hours of abandonment photographic bliss.

By the time we were getting close to wrapping up our photoshoots, I heard the distinct sound of another vehicle approaching. I turned to look and saw a different pickup truck through the trees and brush. It had stopped but then started moving a few minutes later. It then came into full view, which also meant that I was in full view of the occupants. The driver pulled up in front of where I had my tripod set up, exited the truck, and asked me if we had permission to be there. I explained to him that we did and that we had been given permission by two very nice gentlemen in another pickup truck earlier. He lowered his head and shook it a little and instructed me not to go anywhere because he needed to make a phone call. He then got back into his truck and drove it off out of sight back towards where we had entered the property.

I immediately went to go find the others as we had all separated on our own photoshoots at this point. I told them what had just transpired, and we decided it was time for us to leave. We walked toward our vehicles and then noticed that same truck parked there as well. The driver was still inside so we all went to talk with him. We again explained the situation, but he informed us that the property manager was on his way and that we needed to talk with him. As it turned out, the two gentlemen who had earlier given us permission were not authorized to do so. Shortly after, the property manager arrived and was not happy at all with our presence on the property. However, after several minutes of discussion and him realizing that we did indeed feel that we had permission to be there, not to mention the fact that we were not there vandalizing anything, he became calm and pleasant to talk to and allowed us to leave without involving law enforcement. Suffice it to say, I have never returned. I would most definitely advise others who might wish to go against doing so. I have been told that there are cameras up now and it is regularly patrolled.

More buildings from the abandoned renaissance faire.

The castle in the abandoned renaissance faire.

By far the most interesting site I have photographed would have to be the presidents' heads. In 2004, Presidents Park opened in Williamsburg. On display there were the 20-foot tall busts of forty-three presidents of the United States, from George Washington through to George W. Bush. Unfortunately, the park had financial troubles and eventually closed in 2010. A local contractor was hired to demolish the busts, but being a history buff himself, he instead paid to acquire the busts. By early 2013, all of the busts had been relocated to his private property. His hopes had been to somehow find a way to put them on display again for the public to enjoy, but that plan never came to fruition, so there they have sat since 2013, slowly deteriorating.

The decaying busts of George Washington and Andrew Jackson beneath the stars.

Sadly, over the years, many different people have illegally snuck onto his property to see and photograph the busts. Ever since I first discovered the existence of these grand statues several years ago through another's photograph posted to social media, I have honestly felt as if every photographer out there had been to the property and photographed them except for myself.

The presidents' heads.

I was not willing to trespass on this gentleman's property in order to get these shots, so for years, I silently envied those who had photographed them all the while hoping for a legal and legitimate opportunity to do so myself one day. That opportunity finally arrived as I was preparing this book. Another local photographer, who has made quite a name for himself by finding out the histories behind all of the abandoned buildings he has photographed and giving presentations about them all over the state, successfully struck a deal with the gentleman who owns these busts. As a result of this deal, many people, not just photographers, have been able to attend a series of private events hosted by this photographer before these busts disappear from our state forever. I am tremendously grateful for the hospitality of the owner to allow us onto his property to photograph these beautiful busts, and for the photographer who made the arrangements.

The presidents' heads.

The presidents' heads.

The bust of Abraham Lincoln sitting in front of other former presidents of the United States.

I will conclude this book with the image on the following page. Of all the old and abandoned houses or decayed and empty buildings I have seen and photographed over the years, the next one left me feeling much more haunted than any of the others have left me. At first glance, it will not appear any different from the rest of the images within this book. However, the reason I got chills when I stopped to capture it on camera is because once upon a time, I had walked within this building. At the time, it was the home of a friend of mine and her loving family who all lived happily within its walls.

Fast-forward twenty-some years and there I was, on the side of the road with my tripod and camera set up, photographing it as an abandoned building. I guess, when you once, yourself, walked within the walls of a home that is now abandoned, it feels that much emptier and more forgotten, not to mention how it must feel to those who once resided there themselves. Recently, this home was demolished and only a pile of rubble remains where it once stood.

My friend recently shared with me some of the history behind this old building. Once upon a time, it was a store that belonged to her great-great grandparents. It was the first store in the area to have gas pumps. It also had a small kitchen where I am sure the customers of the day were able to satisfy their hunger with homemade treats after having had their cars filled up.

Once again, we have another building that reminds me of that old country store where I worked for three and a half years as a teenager. The memories and experiences had while working there are precious to me along with the memory of the store itself. I feel a little sorry for those who have never had the opportunity to step into an old country store like that with old floorboards creaking beneath your feet, feeling the warmth of the fire burning in the wood stove, and smelling the wonderful scents of freshly made food emanating from the tiny kitchen. Those were simpler times, but they were definitely wonderful times as well.

It is my hope that I will be able to document many more of these old and abandoned buildings through my photos. It is also my hope that we will not forget and abandon those that came before us—those who built the foundations upon which we now stand. Sooner than we wish, they will no longer be among us, and we will have become to the next generation, as they are now to us. That which we now call the present will all too quickly be regarded as history.

May we have a greater appreciation for these decrepit structures and the everyday history that once played out within their walls. May we also, more especially, have a greater appreciation for all those around us, notably those who may have been left alone by society, inadvertently or not.

Just because one may feel abandoned and forgotten does not mean that it is actually so. We have the power to change those types of perceptions for the better. This is my wish.

The old home that once belonged to a friend and her family. Before they lived there, it was a store owned by her great-great grandparents. This building no longer stands.

ABOUT THE AUTHOR

SEAN TOLER is an amateur photographer living in the Richmond, VA, area. He got into photography, so to speak, as soon as he had a 35-mm point and shoot camera as a teenager. He took many a sunrise or sunset photo with it; in fact, he still photographs them to this day. His involvement with abandonment photography began, and remains, something personal for him. As a teenager, his first real job was at an old country store. That country store no longer exists, and unfortunately, he never thought to photograph it. He now hopes that by capturing old buildings such as this on camera, he is helping to preserve part of history as more and more of these old buildings succumb to weakness and decay or are demolished in the name of progress.

Prints of the photos seen in this book, as well as many others can be purchased at his ArtPal website: artpal.com/seantolerphoto

His photos can also be found on his Facebook page: facebook.com/seantolerphoto